The Kids' Career Library™

A Day in the Life of a
Police Officer

Mary Bowman-Kruhm
and Claudine G. Wirths

The Rosen Publishing Group's
PowerKids Press™
New York

Thanks to Jerry Morales and Bruno and the City of Frederick, Maryland, Police Department
for their help with this book.

Published in 1997 by The Rosen Publishing Group, Inc.
29 East 21st Street, New York, NY 10010

First Edition

Book Design: Erin McKenna

Photo Illustrations: Cover and all photo illustrations by Kelly Hahn.

Bowman-Kruhm, Mary.
     A day in the life of a police officer/ by Mary Bowman-Kruhm and Claudine G. Wirths.
          p.   cm. — (The kids' career library)
     Includes index.
     Summary: Describes a day in the life of a police officer and his police dog.
     ISBN 0-8239-5095-6
     1. Police—Juvenile literature. 2. Police dogs—Juvenile literature. [1. Police. 2. Police dogs. 3. Dogs.
     4. Occupations.] I. Wirths, Claudine G. II. Title. III. Series.
     HV7922.B69 1997
     363.2'2'02373—dc21
                                                                                    96-54021
                                                                                       CIP
                                                                                        AC

Manufactured in the United States of America

Contents

Officer Morales and Bruno

The job of the police is to **enforce** (en-FORSS) our laws, protect us, and try to **prevent** (pre-VENT) crime. Jerry Morales is a police officer. Like most police officers, he has a partner who works with him. Unlike most police officers, Officer Morales does not have a person for his partner. He has a big **German shepherd** (JER-mun SHEP-erd) dog named Bruno.

Bruno lives with Officer Morales and his family. The first thing Officer Morales must do every day is to take Bruno for a walk.

◀ Officer Morales and Bruno
start their day with a walk.

At the Station

Officer Morales and Bruno start work at 8:00 in the morning.

First, there is **roll call** (ROLL CALL) at the police station. At roll call, Officer Morales and the other police officers learn what went on in their neighborhoods during the night. They also hear about any problems. Officer Morales learns where he and Bruno will **patrol** (puh-TROL) that day.

Roll call is where Officer Morales learns what he and Bruno will do that day. ▶

Patrol Work

Before they go on patrol, Officer Morales checks his car to be sure it is clean, both inside and out. His patrol car has a wire cage for Bruno, but sometimes Bruno rides in the front seat.

Officer Morales and Bruno ride around town and check that everything is safe. Bruno has been taught to do what Officer Morales says. Bruno can look for lost keys, find drugs, chase people who are running from the police, and search buildings.

◄ Bruno has been taught to do all sorts of things, such as search through buildings for criminals.

A Break-In?

Officer Morales has a police radio in his patrol car. Uh, oh! The **dispatcher** (dis-PACH-er) on the radio says the door of an empty store is open. Has someone broken in? Officer Morales drives to the store to check it out.

"Go," he tells Bruno. Bruno jumps out of the car and runs through the door.

Officer Morales stands by, ready for trouble. He hopes Bruno will not get hurt if anyone is inside.

As soon as Officer Morales tells him to, Bruno heads for the store. ▶

All Is Well

Bruno comes back out of the store. He is wagging his tail. A wagging tail means no one is in the store, and everything is safe. Officer Morales also looks around the store to be sure everything is okay. He calls the dispatcher. "Call the owner of the store and let him know the door is open," he says.

Bruno and Officer Morales get into the car and go back on patrol. Later, Officer Morales will write a report that says they checked the store.

◀ Officer Morales and Bruno check the store together to make sure it is safe.

13

The Fight

Two men have started a fight on a street corner. Their friends join the fight. Lots of other people stop to watch. Officer Morales and Bruno are sent to break up the fight. When they get there, Officer Morales tells Bruno to walk through the crowd of people.

Bruno walks through the people. The crowd breaks up. They forget about the fight. Other police officers move the crowd along.

"Sometimes Bruno does a better job than a police officer could," says Officer Morales.

Officer Morales and his partner head out when the radio tells them where to go. ▶

Another Call

Bzzz. Bzzz. The radio in the patrol car is on again. "There is a car wreck on Park Street at Wood Road," the dispatcher says.

Officer Morales and Bruno drive to the wreck with the siren on and the lights flashing. Officer Morales takes pictures while the **medics** (MED-iks) help the people who were hurt.

"What happened?" he asks the people who saw the wreck. Back at the station he will write a report on what he saw and heard and what he thinks caused the wreck.

◀ Officer Morales takes pictures of a car wreck so he will remember what happened.

Bruno Plays a Trick

While Officer Morales checks the wreck, he leaves Bruno to guard the car. Officer Morales knows that if anyone tries to get into the car, Bruno will bark.

Bruno gets tired of waiting for Officer Morales and wants to play. He turns on the patrol car lights! Bruno has learned to hit the buttons with his paws. When the lights go on, Officer Morales runs back to the car. He **scolds** (SKOLDZ) Bruno, but Bruno knows Officer Morales still loves him.

Bruno does a good job guarding the car, but sometimes he plays tricks on his partner. ▶

School

Sometimes Officer Morales takes Bruno with him when he goes to a school to talk to the children. He tells the children that they should **obey** (oh-BAY) laws, say no to drugs, and play safely. He and Bruno show the children how they work as a team. Bruno likes to show people what he has learned.

Officer Morales himself goes to police school twice a month. He must pass tests every year to show that he knows how to do his job.

◄ Officer Morales and Bruno work very hard at their jobs, but they like to have fun too.

The Job of the Police

Police work is not exciting all the time. It's not always the way it may seem on TV. It can be hard and **dangerous** (DAYN-jer-us) work. Officer Morales and Bruno help people. They work hard to keep people safe from crime.

Officer Morales and Bruno know that their jobs are important. They are proud to serve their **community** (kuh-MYOON-ih-tee). Officer Morales likes helping people, and he loves working with Bruno!

Glossary

community (kuh-MYOON-ih-tee) The people who live in an area.

dangerous (DAYN-jer-us) Not safe.

dispatcher (dis-PACH-er) Person who sends an officer on a call.

enforce (en-FORSS) Making sure that laws are followed.

German shepherd (JER-mun SHEP-erd) A kind of large dog.

medic (MED-ik) A person trained to help someone who is sick or hurt.

obey (oh-BAY) To do what you're supposed to do.

patrol (puh-TROL) To protect a certain street, block, or area.

prevent (pre-VENT) To keep something from happening.

roll call (ROLL CALL) Calling a list of names to find out who is there.

scold (SKOLD) To blame for bad behavior or for something that is done wrong.

Index